Kids of Character

I Can Share

By Maria Nelson

Gareth Stevens Publishing

Please visit our website, www.garethstevens.com. For a free color catalog of all our high-quality books, call toll free 1-800-542-2595 or fax 1-877-542-2596.

Nelson, Maria.
I can share / by Maria Nelson.
p. cm. — (Kids of character)
Includes index.
ISBN 978-1-4339-9034-2 (pbk.)
ISBN 978-1-4339-9035-9 (6-pack)
ISBN 978-1-4339-9033-5 (library binding)
1. Sharing—Juvenile literature. 2. Social skills in children—Juvenile literature. I. Nelson, Maria. II. Title.
BJ1533.G4 N45 2014
177.7—dc23

First Edition

Published in 2014 by
Gareth Stevens Publishing
111 East 14th Street, Suite 349
New York, NY 10003

Designer: Nicholas Domiano
Editor: Kristen Rajczak

Photo credits: Cover, p. 1 Pressmaster/Shutterstock.com; p. 5 Ingram Publishing/Thinkstock.com; p. 7 David Madison/The Image Bank/Getty images; pp. 9, 11 Wavebreak Media/Thinkstock.com; pp. 13, 19 iStockphoto/Thinkstock.com; p. 15 Stockbyte/Thinkstock.com; p. 17 Design Pics/SW Productions/Getty Images; p. 21 Danielle Donders - Mothership Photography/Flickr/Getty Images.

Printed in the United States of America

CPSIA compliance information: Batch #CS13GS: For further information contact Gareth Stevens, New York, New York at 1-800-542-2595.

Contents

Boldface words appear in the glossary.

What Is Sharing?

Sharing is one part of having good manners. Someone who shares lets others use what they have. It shows they care about other people's feelings and needs. While sometimes sharing is hard, it can also be fun!

The Guest Knows Best

Emily **invited** Justin over to play with her new basketball and hoop. Emily liked to shoot baskets! But after she shot the ball once, she let Justin take a turn. Emily can share.

Susie and Hannah were playing with Susie's stuffed animals. Hannah asked to play with Susie's **favorite** bear. Susie liked sharing the bear with Hannah. She wanted Hannah to have fun with a special toy.

Help a Friend

Zeke left his music book for school band practice at home! Zeke's friend Brian sat next to him during practice. Brian offered to let Zeke look at his music book. Brian can share.

Becca thought Luca's book about dogs looked really cool. She asked if she could borrow it, and Luca said yes. She returned the book the next day. Borrowing and sharing are alike. Often, returning something is part of sharing, too!

Sharing Time

Anika planned to spend a whole afternoon with her Aunt Kathy. They had lunch and went to the park. Anika was sharing her time with her aunt. It helped show her aunt how much Anika cared.

Jake and his family have often spent time **volunteering** at the local soup kitchen. They helped make and serve food to people who were hungry. Sharing their time in this way made a difference to a lot of people.

For Those in Need

Isabella had a lot of toys. When her class was collecting toys for needy children, she picked out some she didn't use anymore to **donate**. Sharing her old toys made Isabella feel really good.

DONATIONS

Another Kind of Sharing

Hamma and Dev each had a **chore** to do. They decided to help each other! They thought that by sharing the chores, they would be done faster. Learning to share **responsibilities** can make hard jobs easier—and more fun!

Glossary

chore: task

donate: to give, especially to a cause

favorite: liked best

invite: to ask to go somewhere or do something

responsibility: something a person is in charge of

volunteer: to work without pay

For More Information

Books

Packard, Mary. *Little Raccoon Learns to Share*. New York, NY: Sterling, 2013.

Williams, Sam. *Sharing*. Vero Beach, FL: Rourke Publishing, 2012.

Websites

Be a Volunteer

kidshealth.org/kid/feeling/thought/volunteering.html

Use this website to help you find ways to share your time with those in need.

Kids' Health Topics: Good Manners

www.cyh.com/HealthTopics/HealthTopicDetailsKids.aspx?p=335&id=2526&np=287

Sharing is just a part of having good manners. Learn more about it here.

Publisher's note to educators and parents: Our editors have carefully reviewed these websites to ensure that they are suitable for students. Many websites change frequently, however, and we cannot guarantee that a site's future contents will continue to meet our high standards of quality and educational value. Be advised that students should be closely supervised whenever they access the Internet.

Index